ANGEL SPIRIT GUIDES - PART I

KNOWING AND UNDERSTANDING YOUR
ARCHANGELS USING GUIDED MEDITATION

ADESH SILVA

© **Copyright 2020 - All rights reserved.**

The content contained within this book may not be reproduced, duplicated or transmitted without direct written permission from the author or the publisher.

Under no circumstances will any blame or legal responsibility be held against the publisher, or author, for any damages, reparation, or monetary loss due to the information contained within this book, either directly or indirectly.

Legal Notice:

This book is copyright protected. It is only for personal use. You cannot amend, distribute, sell, use, quote or paraphrase any part, or the content within this book, without the consent of the author or publisher.

Disclaimer Notice:

Please note the information contained within this document is for educational and entertainment purposes only. All effort has been executed to present accurate, up to date, reliable, complete information. No warranties of any kind are declared or implied. Readers acknowledge that the author is not engaged in the rendering of legal, financial, medical or professional advice. The content within this book has been derived from various sources. Please consult a licensed professional before attempting any techniques outlined in this book.

By reading this document, the reader agrees that under no circumstances is the author responsible for any losses, direct or indirect, that are incurred as a result of the use of the information contained within this document, including, but not limited to, errors, omissions, or inaccuracies.

CONTENTS

Introduction	5
1. Let's Get Right Into It - Archangel Gabriel	13
2. Guided Meditation for Archangel Gabriel	16
3. Archangel Michael	25
4. Guided Meditation Script for Archangel Michael	28
5. Archangel Raphael	39
6. Guided Meditation Script for Archangel Raphael	41
7. Final Meditation Script	51
Conclusion	61
References	67

INTRODUCTION

Life can be quite strange sometimes. It can toss you from one side to the other, it can break your connection to your spirituality, and it can make you jump into a large, undeniably evil pool of negativity.

It's understandable how life can so easily get out of control—because without a trained personal strength and balance, there is no command of what happens to the inner self, nor the outer.

It might sound unbelievable, but the way to regain control over feelings and experiences in life is to commit to them. Focusing on the power within and channelling the energies of the Universe can, without a doubt, help to regain balance and withstand the storms.

INTRODUCTION

So, how exactly do you take back what is yours and start regaining control over your body and mind when they are flooded with a negativity that can even manifest into physical pain?

One method is to call on the power of the archangels through meditation. Of course, you can do this individually, especially if your meditative practices are already advanced—but if there is still room to learn and if it is still quite new then it's likely best to use guided meditation to help focus on the parts of you that need reconnection, healing, and blessing from the infinite positive powers of the Universe.

This novel will provide guided meditation sessions meant to help in whatever kind of issues you may be struggling with, from stress and anxiety, to disease and mental health, or just blocks that do not allow you to fully convey your intentions correctly. These guided meditation sessions are here to help you reconnect with the stream of positive energy in the Universe.

Archangels are supernatural beings in the Abrahamic traditions of Islam, Judaism, and Christianity. The word 'archangel' is derived from Ancient Greek and it means, quite literally, "chief angel" according to the Online Etymology Dictionary. So, in military equivalents, all the archangels are generals of their own divisions of angels, each with its own powers and responsibilities.

INTRODUCTION

Although the exact concept is mostly used in Abrahamic traditions, other religions make note of supernatural beings that are remarkably similar to what Christians, Jews, and Muslims call 'archangels'. Most often, these beings are represented with wings and tools that help them fulfill very clear purposes such as healing, communication, helping with childbirth, and so on.

There are seven archangels in total. Two of them, Gabriel and Michael, are frequently referred to as the leaders of the two remaining tribes of Israel, while the other five have representations and stories that are sometimes disputed in sacred texts, but still acknowledged by most Abrahamic traditions (Judaism, Christianity, and Islam).

Raphael, Ariel, Jophiel, Azrael, and Chamuel are all present, to some extent, in the holy books of Abrahamic religions—but what truly helps us understand them and their purpose are gnostic texts. These are considered to be early Christian gospels that were discovered in 1945 in Egypt, at Nag Hammadi. A total of 52 early Christian texts discovered then are now considered to have belonged to a nearby Pachomian, and although they are not always considered part of the official canon, they are important texts for all the Abrahamic religions (Meyer, 2007).

Looking outside of Christianity, Judaism, and Islam, archangels are superior beings of light that help humans

INTRODUCTION

channel energies from the Universe—and that is precisely what this entire guide will focus on.

It is far from me to want to sway you to one religion or another. In the perspective shown in this book, archangels are beings of pure light that move past organized religion and allow you to connect with the vibrations of the Universe, God, and/or Creation, as you choose to see it.

Try not to look at these archangels through the lens of one religion only, but more through the holistic lens of the energies of the Universe more broadly. For example, they do not pertain to Christianity more than Gnosticism, just as they do not pertain to Abrahamic religions more than to other cultures and religious doctrines.

Everyone's life is far from perfect, but by channeling the energies of the archangels, there is a possibility to re-tune ourselves with the light, positive thoughts, and actions that reflect the purity of goodness that flows through both the macrocosm and microcosm.

The first part of *Angel Spirit Guides* will focus on the first three (and perhaps most well-known) archangels: Gabriel, Michael, and Raphael. Each of them will have two dedicated chapters: One to introduce you to them and one to guide you through channeling them in your life.

INTRODUCTION

As you will see, all of these guided meditations focus on each archangel's specific talents and powers. Archangel Gabriel is the Great Messenger, so he will help you communicate better, as well as bring thoughts to life. Archangel Michael is the Great Defender, so he will be the one to support you through the darkness of fear, resentment, and sadness. Archangel Raphael is the Great Healer, so he will be the one to help you heal physical wounds and find your way through mental health problems, right into the light of the Divine.

Although each of these archangels comes with his own vibrations and special powers, you will see that. However, at some point, they are tangential in some respects. Gabriel might be a messenger, for example, but he is also seen as the bearer of childbirth news and as such, he becomes intrinsically connected to Raphael, for example, who is the healer. Likewise, Raphael is a healer at both a mental and physical level, but it is Michael that who guides us through the darkness of pain.

Bringing the powers of all three archangels into your life is one of the best ways to help yourself through times that might not seem that bright when you allow yourself to be swept into the sea of darkness. It might not happen all of the sudden, but little by little, these positive vibrations will settle into your mindset and enable you to stand up to the gathering clouds over your head.

INTRODUCTION

Because, first and foremost, I was once like you. I hid away in the dark, chained by my own self-diminishing beliefs and mindsets. I was anxious all the time, to a point where nothing made sense to me anymore and fear dominated every single second of my life. I was giving myself up into the darkness, waiting for the resolution and the light to come from the outside, unaware that it should have been the other way around.

It was then that I discovered spirituality and all the gifts it brings into the world. Little by little, I started to learn more about meditation, spirituality, and animal spirit guides. It was my knowledge that pulled me through the dark times of my life to help me see the sunrise again.

I left my darkness behind a long time ago. I am now in my 30s and I have two beautiful children. The Universe has been more than generous with me—and as such, I decided to give back the gift that I was once given myself. In time, I learned how to help others like me too. Hundreds of people have walked with me through their minds and found their spring of light in times when nothing ever felt right.

My name is Adesh Silva and I am writing this book because I genuinely want you, my readers, to reap all the benefits of the amazing experiences that have brought me here. My life experience, as well as all the books I have read on these

INTRODUCTION

topics have aided me tremendously in finding my way to the light—and I trust they will help you too.

Thank you for choosing this guide to aid in your balance-building process. I am humbled, grateful, and genuinely joyful for that. However, more than anything, I am hopeful that this experience will be a step into the light.

I genuinely hope these meditations and channeling of the archangels will help in an achievement in peace of mind and balance in life. It is a very strange thing, but knowing how to deal with its strangeness and how to tame its chaos is key to living happily.

Because you deserve nothing less than a happy life! You are a being created in light and love, out of passion and compassion and as such, you are worthy of the most tender, sweet, and beautiful fruits of life itself!

Allow the light to come to you and let yourself become the light of the Divine!

1

LET'S GET RIGHT INTO IT - ARCHANGEL GABRIEL

Lingering between the human and celestial, archangels are spiritual beings who can intermediate between people and the powers that drive the Universe. There are then seven archangels you can call upon in different challenging situations in life.

In Part I of this book, I will discuss: Gabriel, Michael, and Raphael. In Part II, I will elaborate on the remaining four: Ariel, Jophiel, Azrael, and Chamuel.

Archangel Gabriel is one of, if not the most well-known of the seven. He is the Great Messenger of the Divine, which is specifically why he is usually called upon when communication issues arise. As a protector of artists and teachers, Archangel Gabriel helps them to communicate their messages in a clear and powerful way.

In most of his representations, Gabriel arrives with his horn —a symbol of the messages that pass on from the Divine to Earth like a bridge of communication between the two worlds.

Present in most of the Abrahamic religions, Archangel Gabriel is always associated with messages coming from the Divine. In Christianity, he is the one to bring the news to Virgin Mary, delivering the news of her immaculate conception with Jesus of Nazareth, as well as the birth of John the Baptist. In Islam, Gabriel speaks to Prophet Muhammad and the other prophets of the Quran. In some versions of Christianity, Archangel Gabriel is sometimes overlapped with Noah (Burge, 2011).

Since Archangel Gabriel is also associated with prophetic messages, certain branches of Christianity (such as the Church of the Latter Day Saints), consider him to be one and the same as Noah (in his mortal registry). This association is largely due to the prophetic message Noah brought to humans (Ludlow, 1992).

Archangel Gabriel is also considered to be the protector of childbirth and pregnancy—so couples who have been looking to conceive frequently call on his powers to help them achieve in creating a new life.

Last, but not least, those looking to convey messages but are unable to find the words frequently call on the amazing powers of Archangel Gabriel as well. As the Great Communicator between the Divine and the Earth, Gabriel can help people to articulate their power, life, and belief.

Archangel Gabriel is an inspiration, a powerful energy floating through space and time to create bridges of communication between humans and their spirituality. That is why he is often associated with violet, representative of the crown chakra, responsible for how the spirit communicates.

Regardless of whether someone's endeavors are creative, or purely functional for better, clearer, and more compassionate communication, Gabriel is the archangel to call for help. He embraces with the light of the Messenger and as a bearer of Good News, inspires you, and helps to transgress through the communication blocks anyone may be experiencing to discover the true meaning and direction of life.

2

GUIDED MEDITATION FOR ARCHANGEL GABRIEL

Welcome to a guided meditation for the Archangel Gabriel. If guided meditation is a new concept to anyone reading, know that all that there is to do is lay back in a comfortable position on a soft, cozy surface and read these words .

I will guide you through your Archangel Gabriel meditation step by step—all that is needed is deep breaths, and to let yourself be walked through the positive affirmations of Archangel Gabriel. This meditation will help to unlock creativity, communication skills, curiosity, excitement, and innocence to help embrace the beauty and harmony of the world.

Lay down now. Close your eyes, slowly . Find a comfortable position, making sure the back is aligned, the neck is supported, and the feet and hands are soft, as if they are melting into the surface beneath. Feel the texture of the surface being laid on; experience the sensation through your clothes, and sink in deeper to the sensation.

Breathe in and out slowly.

Feel your body holding itself easy, soft, almost as if it were non-physical. Feel the flow of your blood through your arteries, through the little vascularities in your hands and face. Feel how the light touches your entire body, embracing it from head to toe, how it feels on your eyelids and on your arms, how your entire being becomes softer, lighter, like a breeze.

You are now one with the light, because it is from light that you come, and it is in light that you melt. And the light speaks softly to you. Without words, the warmth embracing you now gives you the peace of mind and clarity you have been looking for all along.

You are soft and easy in the way you bear yourself through the material world because you are made of light. And as you become one with the power of the air and luminescence, you start acknowledging your true colors.

The power of the Universe opens your mind to words you never knew, to messages that speak themselves without the need of a human language, with colors and shapes that allow you to pull every single inch of your being—and put it out there, into the world.

You are vulnerable, but fearless. You know your power lies in creating connections and links between humans, between messages, between stories. And as you start to become fully aware of your strengths, you start calling on the power of Gabriel to fully embrace you and give you the energy to move on.

Your inner eye looks towards the sky now. Everything material around you is slowly dissipating and melting into a massive conglomerate, even the way the light feels in your room and the way your clothes feel on your skin. The material world ceases to exist as you open your aura and allow it to blend in with your environment.

And as you open up, you ask Archangel Gabriel to come and help you mend the broken pieces of your communication process, to help you conceive new ideas, or a child, to help you bond with your true self again and start truly speaking your heart out.

Your aura is now ready, open to the endless array of possibilities lying ahead of you. It becomes the light flourishing from your body and soul as they become one, like a waterfall becomes one with the flow of the Universe.

Archangel Gabriel, please come and descend your light upon me and allow me to communicate freely, to say the words I want to say, to send the messages I want to send, to unleash the full power of real love into my work, into my days, into my relationships, and into my dreams.

> *Come bear the great messages of the Divine through me and open me up for the greatness of the infinite compassion of creation. Come help me create life and love and beauty through my body and my spirit.*

> *Help me find the way to create past fear, past blockers, past everything that might have broken my connection to the Higher Messages in the past. Allow me to be the earthly messenger of good faith and good news, just like you are the Heavenly messenger of all that's light and astonishment, all that is positive and good in the cosmos.*

Breathe in deeply and acknowledge this new state of complete and utter relaxation and openness. You are, without any trace of doubt, a child of the Divine. You do not doubt that anymore, because you can feel as your entire self becomes one with the air and the sky and the light of the world.

And as you welcome this new state of your higher self into your life, Archangel Gabriel responds to your call. You can feel the burning of the air as he steps down to give you the support you have been looking for. The space around you becomes warmer and warmer, and a violet light starts to unfold itself in the world that you have embraced.

Gabriel speaks to you in a language you do not know, yet fully understand. He shows you a piece of raw clay and puts it in your hand. From this state of universal bliss you are in, you can feel the fragrance of the clay striking through your entire being, and you can feel the moist, soft texture of this material floating through you.

As Archangel Gabriel lays a hand down on your head, healing your communication chakra, you start feeling your lump of clay getting warmer and warmer. You do not yet know what to do with it, but that is OK because you know you have it in you to mold this clay into the message you want.

The light of Gabriel, the Great Messenger of the Skies embraces you and it merges with your own vibration, bringing it to a higher frequency. Your heartbeat becomes the very rhythm of the entire Universe, the rhythm of the birds flapping their wings and the rhythm of the fields of wheat as they dance in the wind at the end of July.

There is a feeling of coziness and warmth. There is no problem in the world you cannot overcome because you are one with the Divine truth and it speaks through you. This gives a power to mold the clay in the exact shape and form of your soul and of the messages you have been trying to send out for such a long time.

Never before has it been easier for you to trust your inner self, to let it flow through the materials in your hands. You are not only happy about this, but there is an eternal bliss flowing and helping you stay safe on the side of creation.

This is your story. You are molding your own story and message into the world and giving birth to life and ideas as easy as the rivers flow and as softly as cats sleep.

You are one with the rustling of the leaves in fall, the joy and innocence of the first snowflakes, the rebirth of spring and its beautiful pains, and the warmth of the summer revealing itself to humans.

Now more than ever, you can see things clearly, for you have been blessed by Archangel Gabriel with the power to embrace the true life, message, and creative processes that push the world forward into better places.

You know there is pain in the world. but you also know that you can detach from stress and anxiety to allow creativity to heal—yourself first, and then everyone else.

With the help of Archangel Gabriel, know you can bring this light and ease into the lives of loved ones, into the lives of those stumbled upon, and of everyone who opens themselves up to this infinite glory of light and creation.

Your ethereal being is stable in its stance to help the Universe dance through its timeless music. You move in the sounds of the heartbeat of the world, understand everything, and speak softly yet say the truth. You can bring light and life into the world while standing up for yourself and being what the Divine always wanted you to be: An amazing human capable of molding life and creation.

Colors blend into each other, you become one with the light, the world spins in your rhythm and your entire being taps into the music of the cosmos floating through you and allows a channel of communication opened with it.

There is no dream that is untouchable and no life unlivable. There is only eternal bliss, and smoothness. No more blocks, just a sea of beauty navigated with no problem whatsoever.

There is a sense of freedom like birds are free to fly, like the waters of the Earth are to flow in their cycles, and like the mountains are to stand tall and strong. You are a grain of sand and the desert of the Universe at the same time.

Archangel Gabriel is there and his arms embrace you to support a journey every breath of the way. There is power and creation within you as a part of the Divine truth that helps birth beauty into the world of the material to connect the immaterial and humane.

Breathe in deeply and feel the strength given as it travels through your nose, trachea, and lungs, spreading through every inch of your true self.

Breathe out slowly and let all worries, anxiety, and past leave for nothing less than the brilliant light of Creation.

Take this feeling into every day of your life and allow yourself to touch the gorgeousness of creation every second as you move through the physical world.

As you breathe in and out slowly, become aware of your material body again. Know that Archangel Gabriel is guarding you, warming up your space, soul, and life.

You start to slowly feel the room again; the light passing through your windows. Notice the fragrance of the room as it fills your nostrils and awakens you to your physical self and the feeling of the surface underneath the back. The way your fingers feel slightly numb but pleasantly relaxed, just like your entire body.

Breathe in deeply.

Breathe out slowly.

Open your eyes now. You are still one with the Divine light and the creative powers of the Great Messenger, but you can now bring all this into your day-to-day life.

Whatever anxiety there was before you started this meditation is gone now. You feel in control of life and of who you are. The kind of traces you want to leave into the world are understood, and you are empowered to do it as life moves forward.

Thank you for choosing this guided meditation to combat your creative or communicative block. Trust the vibrations felt right now and hold on to them. Come back to this guided meditation whenever the need to recharge with the creative flow of the Universe again.

You are now fully back in your room, ready to take on tasks, dreams, and aspirations. Archangel Gabriel is watching over you, helping you to touch greater messages and understand the real meaning of the cosmos through your work and children.

3

ARCHANGEL MICHAEL

Archangel Michael is a warrior of Heaven and is the general of all archangels and leads them into victory on every occasion. He protects the Gates, and has the power to metaphorically open them.

Archangel Michael is a warrior of Heaven. He is the general of all archangels and leads them into victory on every occasion. He protects the Gates, and he can open them for you.

Perhaps one of the most important wars he fought was that against Lucifer himself. In the Book of Revelation, we are shown that Archangel Michael was precisely the one who led the fight against Satan's forces.

People who call upon the protective energy of Archangel Michael do so when they are feeling restless, blocked, anxious, afraid, or all of the above. Those who suffer from anxiety will find the protective strength of Michael to be a guidance through dark times, as he cuts through the worries and mental pain and allows you to see light and serenity again, perhaps in a more clear way.

Since the fourth century, people have been praying to Archangel Michael for his powers. A powerful presence in the Old Testament, New Testament, Torah, and Quran alike, Archangel Michael lies at the very core of Western spirituality .

As mentioned before, in the Book of Revelation, Archangel Michael is shown as the General of the armies of Heaven fighting off against Satan. In some representations, his defeat over Lucifer is shown as a defeat over a dragon with seven heads, each one representing one of the deadly sins—for example, Albrecht Dure represents him this way in "The Fall of the Rebel Angels".

Different Abrahamic traditions and branches will sometimes perceive Michael differently. He is the advocate and protector of the people of Israel for the Hebrews, the General who defeated Satan in the great War in Heavens for Christians, and Mīkhāʿīl ('Mikhail'), the one responsible for the forces of nature for Muslims (King, 2009).

Even within Christianity, Archangel Michael is sometimes seen differently in Catholicism, the Orthodox faith, and

Protestantism. For example, he is one of the four archangels recognized by Methodists. Some protestants also believe that he is the pre-incarnation version of Jesus Christ (Lees, 1939).

Archangel Michael is frequently associated with healing as well, but not necessarily in the sense of healing a mental or physical ailment, but in healing different people from ties of their past holding them back and not allowing them to fulfill their destiny or ambitions.

Not only is Archangel Michael a great warrior of the spiritual world, but he represents the defense of everything good in creation. That is why he is not only associated with strength and protection, but also with healing and positive energy. He is a seeker of deep truths and has the power to heal minds, bodies, and spirits.

Grief, addiction, depression, physical ailments, loss of faith, breakups—Michael is always there to protect people from falling into shadow. It is perhaps for this reason that Archangel Michael is so frequently represented with a sword as he is there to fight darkness with light, lies with truth, and pain with goodness.

Our guided meditation for Archangel Michael will, thus, focus on letting go and learning how to remove the blockers that give you anxiety or make you feel uneasy and unsafe.

4

GUIDED MEDITATION SCRIPT FOR ARCHANGEL MICHAEL

Welcome to your guided meditation to help you call on the protective forces of Archangel Michael, the one who cuts ties with the negative and helps you tap into the all-powerful positive vibrations of the Universe.

Archangel Michael is the most powerful of the archangels, and calling on him will help you defeat one of the darkest, most terrible issues that can plague your vibrations: fear. Not only that, but Michael can also help you open your heart and your mind to the powers that unlock you and allow you to move forward. Whatever ties you might have with the past or with fears that do not allow you to progress, this guided meditation will help you unleash your glory and your candor into the world and become the success you were destined to be.

For this meditation, I would like to invite you to find a comfortable space to lie down. It can be your bed, a mattress, or a reclining chair that allows you to feel your entire length body in contact with the surface you're on.

Also, I want you to make sure that you will not be distracted for the next minutes. This guided meditation will not take long, but I need you to focus solely on my voice for the entire duration of it. This will allow you to fully immerse in your own energy and call on the Great Defender of Goodness, Archangel Michael, the one who won over the dragon.

Lie down, stretching your feet forward, arms softly placed to your side, palms facing up. Close your eyes and start breathing in and out slowly. Take your time on this. There is no rush. There is nothing to be afraid of right now. There is nothing pushing you. Nothing to take you away from this state of here and now that you are slowly inducing yourself into.

You deserve this and you are worthy of everything this guided meditation will bring upon you with the help of Archangel Michael. Whoever you are and whatever the reason for your blocks or fears might be, this is the beginning of a better connection between you and your inner self, as well as the outer Universe flowing through the energies surrounding you.

That's it. With your eyes closed, gaze through the thin veil of physicality that embraces you. Your body is a precious vessel meant to help you bring about your destiny and fulfill your dreams, ambitions, and goals. Treat it candidly by allowing it to relax entirely. Let go of thoughts that pull you back. Let go of pains that might make you feel afraid of the greatness of the future. Just... let go of your physical self and allow it to fully immerse into a state of well-being.

Breathe in deeply, as deeply as your lungs can hold air in them.

Breathe out slowly, taking your time with every second and enjoying the process you are moving through.

Allow your entire self to relax. Your thoughts are soft, your body is slowly melting into the surface underneath you, feeling its texture and moving past it. You are so relaxed that you almost feel liquid.

You flow through the space around you, almost ethereally unphysical, as you get more and more connected with your spirit and the entire power of the Universe.

You don't feel your body anymore, you only feel the vibrations of your room; listen to my voice as it guides you through a state that opens your entire being to receive the gifts of the Divine through the immense power of the strongest archangel of all: Archangel Michael.

You flow through the room. Like a river on a summer day, you flow outside of your physical space and discover that your spirit can travel anywhere through the wavelengths of your energy.

You become one with the river that moves unencumbered, unaltered. You move through the hurdles and the rocks of the mountains in spring, you flow through the peace of hot summer days in the fields of golden wheat, you open your ears to the rustling winds and crunching leaves of fall, you keep your warmth through your winter flow.

Nothing can stop you. As the river that has been flowing for millennia, you cannot be held back. You follow your own course, the course the Divine has created for you, the path you were always meant to walk.

And as you flow through everything—space and time—you reach a high cliff from whence you can fall. Nothing holds you back because you know that, even though letting yourself go over the cliff could be terrifying, you have the protection of the Divine to guide your steps through this.

And you fall. And in your fall you create a spectacular waterfall that amazes. You shine bright in the sunlight and sing about the nature of the Universe as you flow downwards to reach a new beginning.

You are the river, forever and for always. In you lies the power to not only find your own path, but also walk it. Day and night, through all the seasons that bless the face of Earth and through all the cycles that move through the Universe, you are an unstoppable force that follows its path.

Knowing this opens you to the unending power of the Divine. As a force that flows forward no matter the obstacles, you call on Archangel Michael, the sword bearer who will help you cut ties with your blockers once and forever. Darkness, fear, and anxiety will just cease to exist and you will always be able to come back to this place of free-flow to fuel your growth, your success, and your bright future.

Archangel Michael, hear my call and come upon me to help me allow myself to let go from that which hurts me and stops me from growing into the being God intended me to be.

Come and reveal your strength to me and cut me off from everything that is holding me back. My fears, my darkness, my lost confidence, my lack of energy to go on—cut me back from them and release me as a being of pure love and light into the world.

I am responsible for my own actions, but with your

help, I can move the mountains I was always meant to move. I can be the full, successful, accomplished person I was brought into the world to be.

Archangel Michael, give me your great protection to stand up to the evil lurking from within me, as well as the evils lurking from outside of me. Fight alongside me in this battle against negative vibrations and unleash the chains of my anxiety to let me fly freely, as I am meant to be.

Your vibrations are now fully aligned with those of Archangel Michael, for you call him not in despair, but in full knowledge that his help is there to support you, just like the Earth supports the flow of the rivers through mountains, fields, seasons, days, and night, unimpeded by space and time, but only following their destiny.

And Archangel Michael responds to your call. His stunning royal blue light descends on you and fills your room, your life, your entire self with the glory of the Divine protection, with the strength of the unbreakable shield, with the decisiveness of the sword that defended the dragon.

The grandeur of Archangel Michael overwhelms you, but not in any way that is terrifying or dark. His light embraces you the way silk embraces the naked body: soft, flowing through your pores and enabling you to feel the luxuriousness of his blue light.

And as you look in awe at this magnificent sight and feel the warmth of the Divine embracing you, your connections with the negativity of the past are growing out of you like cords. Archangel Michael takes out his sword and cuts these away from you, detaching you from everything low-vibrational that could have been pulling you back in your efforts to move onwards.

Just like that. With the mighty power he has been bestowed upon by the Divine Grace, Michael disconnects you from anything negative that might pull you back from the path of light you want to walk on.

Your river-like state, flowing through obstacles and seasons, becomes a permanence now. Nothing will ever be able to hold you back. Within you lies an immense power to jump over any kind of obstacle. People who hold you back with their negative energy, events that drag you back in the past, present pains that cloud your vibrations and interrupt your communication with your own flow of abundance and success—they are all gone now.

You are fully aware that they might come haunting you again, but with the strength of the Great Defender,

Archangel Michael, you have trust that you can move past these problems in any way you want.

You are the one flowing through issues and conquering the heights of the cliffs. Your spirit rises above challenges and fights fear with a sword of light forged by the strength of the Great Defender himself.

There is power in enlightenment and positive vibrations and you are now more aware of this than ever. Your mind is open, ready to receive the blessing of the Divine and the guidance of Archangel Michael.

The dark can never hold on to you for long because you have an endless stream of vigor, courage, and stability. No matter what kind of dangers are lurking out in the dark, you have with you a torch more vibrant than the sun itself: Your inner core of vitality, shining through obstacles and helping you rise above challenges.

Archangel Michael's royal blue light is bestowed upon you, giving you the passion you need to fight off the anxiety, the fortitude to move past physical hurdles, and the mental balance to embrace the amazing future that is to come.

You have LIFE running through every single cell of you and LIFE will help you fight to the happy ending you are so worthy of. Your eyes are filled with determination, your thoughts are fully calibrated with the positivity of the

Universe, and your body is ready to support your goals through the times ahead of you.

Darkness is a passing state from now on. It can never linger on. It can never take over. It can never put you down. It can never fight you off. It can never chain you ever again.

You are grateful for all the support and guidance you receive from Archangel Michael and his protective powers. From now on, you are ready. Your mind is trained to vibrate with everything good in the cosmos and allows you to create a lifetime of pure joy, success, and high vibrations.

As you begin to become fully aware of all this, Archangel Michael smiles softly upon you and lifts his wings in all their glory. He will always be there for you, as a guiding presence in your life to hold your hand through fear and darkness and give you light and strength to walk through anything bad that might come your way.

His blue light dims down around you now, but from within you explodes a whole new type of brightness—one that's sourced in your compassion, your love of life, and your belief in the fact that you can do anything you set your mind to.

And as the space around you becomes solely yours again, you start to feel the scent of the room with your renewed senses. You hear my voice loud and clear as it guides you back to your personal physical space.

The surface underneath you begins to make sense all over again. It could be your bed linens or the soft texture of the mattress you're on—whatever it is, you start to really feel it now as you begin to regain your senses and acknowledge your physical presence.

You start to move your fingers a little. They feel slightly numb now, but that's OK. It's just a sign that you are coming back to your physical self, ready to take over the world with your goals, your dreams, and your passions.

YOU are a being made out of light, and you now know this. Pain, fears, sadness—they are passing states through this body of Divine truth that you are now. Your gaze is soft as you begin to fully regain physical consciousness and wrap yourself around the undeniable realism of your inner core of strength.

Breathe in deeply. Take your time; you are back again, with renewed forces, ready to battle anxiety and depression, stress and financial hurdles, worries and negativity.

Exhale slowly and let go of all the things that had held you back before. Archangel Michael has cut you off from all those negative roots and has given you the freedom to make your own choices, unaltered by pessimistic views and ideas.

Open your eyes. Everything around you is bathed in a whole new light now—because you are now aware that you are in control of how you *feel* about everything that comes your way.

You are now aware of just how amazing the power of the Divine leads you to your dreams and aspirations, and how great the support of Archangel Michael is.

Thank you for embarking on this journey with this guided meditation. I hope you will find your peace in it and your power to conquer whatever stands in the way of you being genuinely happy.

5

ARCHANGEL RAPHAEL

Although lesser known than Archangel Michael and Archangel Gabriel, Archangel Raphael is an important angelic presence in our lives—one that is recognized in most of the Abrahamic traditions (Christianity, Islam, and Judaism alike).

As one of the most powerful angels, Raphael can guide you through pain and disease, through hurdles that cause you immense aches at a physical or at a mental level. He is seen as the Great Healer.

If Archangel Michael is frequently represented with a sword that wards off evil and Archangel Gabriel is commonly seen as the bearer of messages through his horn, Archangel Raphael is sometimes represented either with a staff (for his guidance powers) or standing on a fish (as a symbol of his healing powers). In Islam, Archangel Raphael is described as extremely tall (reaching the Heavens with his head and the Earth with his feet) and possessing four wings (Lewis, 2008).

Raphael is present in some branches of Christianity and Judaism in the Book of Tobit as a healer, but he also appears in Islam, where he is a venerated archangel. In Islam, Raphael is the one who will blow through his trumpet when the Day of Resurrection comes. Even more, the same tradition cites him as a great performer of music and speaker of more than a thousand languages (which brings his healing and guidance powers quite close to those of Gabriel).

Archangel Raphael holds within him the power of life and healing both at a physical and at a spiritual level. He is the Great Healer and the Great Guide of the Lost. In his Heavenly hierarchy, Raphael is also the intermediator between other archangels and God.

Raphael is your guide through painful times and your protector when faced with pain of any source, so the guided meditation for Raphael will focus on helping you call on him for his healing powers at a physical and a psychological level.

6

GUIDED MEDITATION SCRIPT FOR ARCHANGEL RAPHAEL

Hello and welcome to your guided meditation for Archangel Raphael. As we move through a meditative state, I will only ask two things of you: To allow your entire being to relax and to follow my voice as we proceed on this journey together.

Find a place where you can lie down comfortably—such as your bed or a mattress. You will be here for the following minutes, so it is quite important that your back, neck, and limbs are all properly supported and cozy.

Once you have laid down, close your eyes slowly and start breathing in deeply. Inhale. And exhale. Breathe in. And breathe out. Let it all happen slowly, like the movement of the clouds on summer days.

This will be your rhythm for the entire duration of this guided meditation. Fall into it and feel its beat. Allow yourself to sink deeper into your inner self and, from there, summon all the faith and power within you to call on Archangel Raphael, the Great Healer of the World.

Think, for a second, of the things that pain you. It might be a physical pain, illness, disease, or an emotional pain, like trauma, depression, anxiety, or stress. Whatever it is, I want you to focus this entire guided meditation on the specific point that hurts and allow it to mend, heal, and recharge with positive energy.

All the healing begins with a deep breath. Take a very deep breath and exhale it just as slowly. Don't rush, there is absolutely no reason to move through this at a pace that's in any way higher than what your breath dictates right now.

Healing begins here and now, within you, through the power of the Divine. As you listen to my voice, you will plunge deeper into your entire being and allow your chakras to open to the message and strength of the Universe unleashing all the beauty, power, and love within you. And that's when you will be able to start healing from whatever pain you have been going through.

Listen to my voice and breathe slowly. Your body is comfortable and soft. Your gaze is soft. Your breathing is soft. Everything feels like melting. Your entire mind is easy, your inhales and exhales are easy, the way you feel right now, right here, lying on your surface is easy as well.

You melt into your space and allow yourself to let go of all the stress, all the tension, all the strain in your muscles and in your mind. This moment is yours and nobody can take this away from you.

And as you relax deeper and deeper and follow my voice, your spiritual self lifts from the chains of the physical realm. You are still aware of your body and the amazing things it does for you—but for the moment, you need to see yourself from the outside a little and travel through the channels of the Universe to re-discover your essence.

Everything is easy now. Stress and pain simply do not exist because you have lifted yourself from everything physical and you are allowing yourself to see things clearly, from the perspective of pure energy.

Let the sounds flow through every inch of your body. Let this state of infinite bliss embrace you the way summers embrace the heat of the sun and the way love embraces the power of change.

Think of what used to ache you. What body part was in pain? What part of your mind was burning with anxiety and negativity? How did all this make you feel as a whole?

And how does it feel now that you have let it all go and enabled your being to reconnect with the true essence of what you are, of what God made you to be, of what the Universe built you as?

And as you begin to become more aware of how easy it is to let go and allow yourself to just *be*, you feel open to call on the infinite love of Archangel Raphael, the Great Healer of the skies.

You call on him the way you do with someone you are genuinely fond of now.

> *Archangel Raphael, come and guard over me and give me the strength to take this infinite state of bliss and painless existence into my day-to-day life.*
>
> *Allow me to be one with the powers that have created me. Allow me to live through the worst and get to the other side victorious and enlightened. Allow me to take your love and protection into the world for myself, for my family, for all the people I love—and beyond.*
>
> *Give me the strength to move mountains and the softness to accept that I am human in all my being,*

with every inch of who I am, with every breath I take and give back into the world.

Give me the self-love to accept that all pain is temporary and that healing starts from within myself, within the light I am made of, within my inner essence as it flows through my body cells, my mind, and my every breath.

Give me the wisdom to accept I am here for a reason and for a purpose and that my pain, mental or physical, is nothing but a small burden compared to the pain of my brethren—a burden I can release myself from through the touch of your protective healing.

Archangel Raphael responds to your call and descends to bless you with his energy. As he gets closer to you, the room fills with golden light. It feels warm and good like a sunrise near the ocean, like the first days of spring after a cold winter, like the warmth of a fireplace burning through the nights of cool weather.

The golden light grows on you and on the space around you, and although the feeling of this infinite warmth is familiar, you know you have never felt anything quite like it before. The gold feels more precious, more powerful, and more illuminated than anything ever experienced by human beings.

The Divine power of Archangel Raphael descends upon you, upon your opened self, upon your thoughts and upon your physical body. The room in which you find yourself right now becomes the center of everything good in the Universe as the light of Raphael continues to grow into every corner of your internal and external space.

Your soul is ready to receive the love and the healing powers of the greatest Archangel in Heaven and beyond. He smiles down on you the way a parent smiles down on his children as they start getting better after sickness. His sword in his sheath, Archangel Raphael lifts his hands and places them over you, allowing the blissfulness of the Divine to fully wrap you in its warmth and state of well-being.

You feel complete. You now feel there can never be anything bad in your life, for there are Divine powers working to protect you, those you love, and those you yet do not know to love.

You feel like everything is just pure beauty and goodness, for in the presence of the Great Defender of the Skies, you cannot feel anything else other than the power of God as it protects those who believe in the positive lights of his Creation.

You know that this energy you feel right now is absorbed into the physical body lying down on the floor or on the bed and you know that you can take this into your days, into your weeks, into your years and carry it with you through life like a shield of protection against everything negative.

Pain simply does not exist any longer. The places that used to ache are now soft and enlightened, the self-loathing that might have troubled your mind has now disappeared, the sadness is all gone.

And you are left as a pure being of light, embraced by the protection of Archangel Raphael the Divine Healer. You open your soul to receive the nectar of his remedial energy and let it flow through your being.

Pain may come, but you now know that it will always go away because you have the protection of the Great Healer to watch over you as you move about your days and your years.

Raphael smiles down on you once more. You are worthy of the love of the Divine, you are worthy of the healing and abundance this brings with it. Whatever place in your life was in pain, whatever issues you might have had with being disconnected from the flow of abundance in your life—they are all gone. Raphael helps you mend your connections with your being, your higher self, and the flow of goodness in the world.

And as you feel his power running through your bloodstream, ready to fix what was broken and ready to shield you from future pain, you become more aware of your physical body again.

You get closer to the body lying down in your room and embrace it with all the love of the Divine you have received. Even though this state of pure relaxation will end soon, you know you can take that energy and bring it into your day to day life to heal your wounds and open a permanent channel of communication between YOU and the UNIVERSE's positive energies.

Your body starts to feel yours again. You start to feel like you have control over what pains you and what doesn't. You start to feel like you can master your thoughts and channel them into positive vibrations whenever you feel down or disappointed.

Life is never a perfect path, but you now have the strength of Archangel Raphael to guard over you in times of pain and trouble. Your inner gaze is peaceful and filled with the warmth of Divine love and that will help you move past all hurdles, all stress, and all physical pain that might ever come your way.

Your body is yours again now. You start feeling your breaths going through your nose and through your lungs again. You start feeling the texture of the surface you're lying upon again. You start experiencing the room temperature again. And you begin to feel your eyes moving ever so slightly, your fingers tingling a little, and your feet as they lie stretched out on the floor.

Your life becomes yours again, but in a different light—one that is golden with the healing energies of Archangel Raphael and his fondness of everything good and just in the world.

Breathe in deeply and feel the oxygen filling your lungs and moving through your bloodstream to energize you.

Breathe out slowly and feel the pain go away, little by little. It is now but a memory of the past and something you will always be prepared for in the future.

Listen to my voice as I am taking you back to your room, your body, your life. Start to slowly move your fingers again.

Open your eyes.

You are now back in your room, filled with the energy of goodness and healing, ready to take over problems because Archangel Raphael is always there, with you, to help you jump obstacles and heal everything that aches, with every breath you take.

The point that pained you before starting this guided meditation is now relaxed and softened. Whether it was physical pain or psychological, you are now fully aware of your own power to generate positive vibrations strong enough to help you move through pain and reach the end of the tunnel to see the light.

Battling any kind of disease, mental or physical, can feel, indeed, tiresome. But with your inner core now shielded against negative energy and with Archangel Raphael protecting you from all evil, you now have all the tools you need to win and show yourself victorious on the other end of this struggle.

Because struggle is nothing but a human construct, and when you tap into the healing powers of the cosmos with the help of the Great Healer, you access all its rejuvenating, curative powers.

Take this newfound or restrengthened belief in the power of the Good into your day and win over everything that troubles you. As a being made of light, your vibrations can only resonate with the most blissful, loving energies of the Universe.

7

FINAL MEDITATION SCRIPT

Archangels Gabriel, Michael, and Raphael are, as I was saying earlier, among the most well-known of the archangels. Together, they help you move through blockages of any kind. They might be of an artistic nature, for example, if you cannot create with your words, your hands, or your mind. They might be of a health-related nature, if pain is blocking you from moving on. Or they might be of a fear-related nature, if anxiety is crippling your energy.

These archangels have the purpose of guiding you through your unblocking process from different perspectives. While they might not do the work *for* you, they can definitely help you channel the right vibrations and create bridges with the energy of the Divine, of the Eternal Universe.

In this final meditation script, I will guide you through the channeling of all four remaining archangels and their powers: Ariel, Jophiel, Azrael, and Chamuel, whose powers come together to help you battle external forces, as well as support your internal core of strength.

For this guided meditation, I am inviting you to lie down comfortably on a surface you like—your bed or a Yoga mat, perhaps. Stretch out your legs and leave your arms soft by your side, palms facing up.

Close your eyes. This is your time to rejuvenate and heal yourself from the negativity of external forces, so make sure your phone is shut down and that you have the following minutes all to yourself.

There's nobody else in this room but you and my voice. Listen carefully and follow through the steps, as I will be guiding you through a journey that will help you refresh your spirit and your body.

Breathe in deeply. Take your time here, nobody is rushing you into anything. You are all by yourself, listening to the sounds surrounding you and my voice. Feel the fragrance of your room going through your nostrils and into your body. Slowly shift this scent to a fragrance you love and cherish. It's a familiar scent, maybe. Something that reminds you of comfort, coziness, and peaceful evenings of winter spent by the fireside. Or it might be something that reminds you of the beach, of sand and hot skin bathing in the sunlight. Whatever scent surrounds you right now, let it take over and fuel your energies.

Exhale slowly. Take your time with this as well. As you breathe out the air of your room and prepare to inhale through your favorite scent again, you dive deeper into yourself. To channel the power of the four archangels, you will first have to let go of your physical self, with its pains and its strains, with how the skin feels right now and how the surface underneath you is warming up under your body.

Breathe in.

And breathe out.

You are slowly becoming one with your environment—one with your favorite scent, one with the memories it brings along. You are now slowly melting into everything that surrounds you and leaving your physical body to rest as you get ready to recharge your mind and start anew with a fresh perspective on whatever it is that is troubling you.

That's it. You are pure energy at this point and as a being not bound by the physicality of your body now getting the rest it deserves, you can travel anywhere. As such, you allow your favorite scent to take you to a beautiful memory of it.

Let your imagination run on this scent and take you to a very happy place you feel like you belong to. It could be the fireplace in your grandparents' house on Christmas Eve. It could be a bonfire you started with your friends when you were out camping as a teenager. It could be a beach you visited once and felt happy at. Go there. Go where your memory takes you and follow the lead of this happy memory.

Immerse yourself fully in it. Feel the temperature on your skin. Is it cold? Is it cozy because there's a fire? Maybe it just feels like the first rays of sunlight in spring, or like the dashing sun of August. Maybe it just feels good—the perfect balance between warmth and coolness.

How is the light surrounding you? Is it at dawn? Maybe it could be nighttime already. Or it could be in the middle of the day, as you lie down on the beach and savor the salty air.

How do your feet feel? Are they deep, buried in hot sand, or do they feel cozily wrapped in thick socks? Are you wearing something on your feet, even? Feel the texture of what you are wearing, if there is something covering your feet, or feel the texture of the ground beneath you if you are barefoot.

What do you hear? How does it all come together in music? Is it a nice, quiet day with maybe, just some background relaxing music? Or maybe your grandpa is telling a story somewhere in the other room? Perhaps you hear seagulls and the ocean?

Create this entire landscape of your memory right now and allow yourself to be fully embraced by it, in this moment of utter relaxation. Open your mind to the beauty of this moment, of the *here and now* that always makes you happy.

Open your chakras to receive the positive vibrations of this moment. Allow them to absorb the energy of the Good in the Universe through this happy memory of yours. Allow them to fully open themselves to the Powers of Creation.

You can feel your entire body surrounded by Divine energy now. It's not of a clear color just yet—just pure light, shining bright through you and flowing from the top of your head and into every area of your body. It lingers on in the heart chakra, filling it with Divine love, and then travels through your bloodstream to all the other parts of your body.

And as you feel this light, this pure form of energy flowing through your being, you call upon Archangel Ariel. As the Great Protector of Nature, he feels good here, with you, in your memory. He can sense you love animals and plants and that, in one way or another, you have brought them with you in your happy place; through the ocean guarding the beach or the sounds of the wood behind your bonfire, through the rustling of the winter wind outside as you sit by the fireplace, or through the fragrance of the spring as you walk through a park.

You ask Archangel Ariel to bestow upon you the power of rejuvenation, just like spring bestows its power of rebirth on the plants and animals of Earth. And Ariel reaches his hands and blesses you with the protection of everything living under the Sun.

You are grateful for this gift and feel more energized than ever. As such, you are now ready to call upon Jophiel, the Great Protector of New Ideas. Whatever point in life you might be at right now, Jophiel will enable you to find your way through your problems and come forward with truthful, functional solutions.

Jophiel descends upon you and takes a seat by Ariel, opening his arms to embrace you in the energy of new beginnings, the enthusiasm and joy of fresh ideas, and the power of making them come true.

You are now awestruck with so much positive energy you almost feel like flying. Obstacles have nothing on you, regardless of whether they are external or internal. Ariel's natural rejuvenation and Jophiel's vibration for novelty are pushing you through this time in your life and giving you the strength you need to be successful.

And as you acknowledge the gratitude running through your entire being right now, you call upon Archangel Azrael, the Great Protector of New Beginnings. As the one to help the dead pass into their new state, Azrael can also help you move through from your current state of mind to a state of mind that's focused, productive, and shielded from any kind of external negative emotions.

Azrael comes and takes a place near his brothers, pushes his palm forward and releases his Divine light of change to channel through your chakras and your personal core of light and balance.

You feel like you can move mountains now. Nobody can stop you. No negative people in your life can take this away from you because all this, happening right here and right now, is *here forever*, within YOU, in a place that nobody can reach.

Your immense gratitude calls upon the last, but not the least significant of the archangels: Chamuel, the Peace Bringer. No matter how much natural rejuvenation force you might have, no matter how many amazing new ideas you might be gifted with, and no matter how ready you are for change, it all means nothing if you don't do it with peace of mind.

And that is precisely why Chamuel is here for. The one archangel power to connect all dots and help you move through changes and achieve success with peace of mind is here to protect you from rout and noise, from overwhelming negative vibrations that might take you off course.

He embraces you with immense love and compassion, giving you the feeling that you have finally reached a point where all the negative voices shut down entirely and allow you to BE the destiny you have been given.

You turn to each of the archangels and smile to them. They smile back as they slowly fade away from your happy place, leaving their energetic trail behind—and the seed of their power deeply buried in your core of strength.

You have never felt more grateful for the chances life has given you. You have never felt more empowered to follow your dreams. You have never felt more that the entire nature surrounding you is conspiring to make you *whole* from every point of view.

With the powers of these four archangels guarding over you, actions are nothing but a consequence of your mind. What you create in your mind is what becomes reality in the immediate physicality of your life. What you think is what you create. What you breathe through is what you end up inhaling back in.

You are now energized with the fortitude of Divine Mother Nature, Fresh Ideas, Power to Change, and Peace of Mind to connect everything and guide you through sane decisions.

And as you acknowledge all this, you start to slowly come back to your room. The scent of your happy memory still lingers on, but it starts to blend in with the real scent of your space. Your gaze becomes more focused with every second, and your body starts to regain full control and consciousness. Your fingers start to move, your toes feel just a little bit tingly, your nose breathes in the air of your room.

Open your eyes. Take this feeling of *"everything is possible"* into your life with every minute and walk through your new beginnings and old problems with the balance of the four archangels guarding over you.

Take control of your future, in the light of the Divine that's now flowing through you. Everything is, indeed, possible!

CONCLUSION

Some may say guided meditations are nothing but make-believe. After all, they're just words, right?

And yet, the power of words is already well-documented. From the Christian Genesis, where we are clearly told that *"in the beginning, there was the Word"* (John 1:1, NIV) to the effects words have on masses in modern times (for the better *and* for the worse), we have been proven, time and again, that words have their own mystique.

Even more than that, scientific research shows that meditation *is* actually effective. According to a study run in 2015, meditation can help relieve not only symptoms of stress, but also alleviate symptoms of epilepsy, menopause, premenstration, anxiety, and other ailments (physical or mental) (Sharma, 2015).

CONCLUSION

And that's just *one* study out of tens, hundreds, maybe thousands of research papers that reach the same conclusion: Meditation *works* on all grounds. It might not be fully explained why or how exactly, but most scientists and medical doctors can agree that meditation does, indeed, help on multiple grounds.

Words really do matter. They are the "programming language" our brain uses, so it makes all the sense in the world that words can make a major difference in pretty much anyone's life.

The way you speak to others can influence not only your message per se, but also how you are perceived out there, in the world. The way you speak to yourself, however, reprograms your mindset and projects in the exterior in how you feel, how you react to the events in your life, and how you interact with other people. It's all a cycle, and it starts within you: With how you speak to yourself and how you allow yourself to absorb positive self-talk.

Guided meditations are meant to help you with that. Yes, they can definitely help you detach and relax. And yes, they can definitely help you focus better. But beyond anything else, guided meditations like the ones in this book help you create a mental landscape that fosters growth, peace, and light through the power of words.

CONCLUSION

Channeling the archangels to help you in this journey is a powerful tactic to help yourself reinforce your affirmations and truly embed them into your mental 'code'. Changing from a life of stress, pain, and anxiety to a life of blissful balance begins with one small step: Breathing in deeply and inhaling words of empowerment while calling upon Divine guides like Archangel Michael, Gabriel, or Raphael.

In times of fear and darkness when anxiety and depression take over, Archangel Michael will help you cut ties with your blockers and release you as a free being, capable of conquering the underlying darkness of your imagination.

In times of sickness, mental or physical, Archangel Raphael will come to help you find the power within you to heal and start over. It could be mental unbalance, it could be a physical health issue—whatever it is, you can trust on the Divine touch of Raphael to heal and mend the broken pieces and help you become whole again.

In times where words have no meaning and you are unable to create (in an artistic or perhaps very physical way), Gabriel will come to help you create bridges of communication between your mind and life itself.

You have to believe in the power you have to change for all this to work, though. Yes, channeling the archangels will undoubtedly help you and give you the spiritual support you

CONCLUSION

need so much. But ultimately, they will only act as guides through the dark woods of what's troubling you in the present. They will be your mentors and your support, your parents and your friends, your guardians and your source of Divine love.

But at the end of the day, YOU are the one who will pull yourself through. Spiritual help is there just as an aid, not as a means by which you can achieve success. Without it, your journey is bound to be a lot harder not because you are 100% dependent on spiritual guides, but because their energy helps you vibrate the right way.

You have to do the hard work. You have to wake up every day and face the demons. You have to battle the fear and anxiety. You have to fight through the pain that cripples your mind and your body. You have to break through the blocks that are holding your creative force back. YOU are the gifted being capable of truly pulling yourself out of these dark times.

It's just that doing it with the archangels by your side will feel more natural, a little easier, and a lot more like a fully supported process. Look at it this way, if you want. If you walk through the desert with just a small amount of water in your bottle, you may or may not find your way to your destination. But if you walk through the desert with an endless supply of hydration sourced in the Divine itself, you have all the chances to succeed.

Nobody can promise you this will be easy. But as you move through every second, every minute, and every hour of every day with the energy of the archangels by your side, you will discover that life means a lot more than just darkness, fear, and pain.

You will accept yourself more, open yourself more to the positive vibrations of the cosmos, and find it easier to search for your inner core of peace, balance, and strength even through the darkest times.

In Part II of *Angel Spirit Guides*, we will talk a little more about the other four archangels: Ariel, the Great Protector of Nature, Jophiel, the Great Protector of Artists and Beauty, Azrael, the Great Protector of Passings and Grievers, and Chamuel, the Great Protector of Forgiveness. Just like the first three archangels introduced and channeled in Part I of this series, the remaining four archangels have powers that are tangential at a certain level—as it was shown in Chapter 7 here as well.

I hope with all my heart that this guide has helped you find at least a little bit of peace and love in your life and that it will continue to be a resource for you in times of turmoil—internally and externally.

CONCLUSION

If you liked the book and the guided meditations, please do not hesitate to leave a review. I read each and every single one of them because each and every single one of the people who choose to follow through their mindset-changing processes is amazingly important to me. As such, their opinions help me create better content, that speaks to them more, and, ultimately, *helps them* more as well.

REFERENCES

Burge, S. (2011). *Angels in Islam: Jalal al-Din al-Suyuti's al-Haba'ik fi Akhbar al-malik.* Routledge.

Encyclopedia Britannica. (n.d.). *Michael | Description, history, & feast days.* Encyclopedia Britannica. https://www.britannica.com/topic/Michael-archangel.

Lewis, J. R., Oliver, E. D., & Kelle S. S. (2008). *Angels A to Z.* Visible Ink.

Online Etymology Dictionary. (2020). *Archangel | Origin and meaning of archangel by Online Etymology Dictionary.* Etymonline.com. https://www.etymonline.com/word/archangel.

REFERENCES

Sharma, H. (2015). *Meditation: Process and effects.* AYU (An International Quarterly Journal Of Research In Ayurveda), 36(3), 233. https://doi.org/10.4103/0974-8520.182756

www.ingramcontent.com/pod-product-compliance
Lightning Source LLC
Chambersburg PA
CBHW071408070526
44578CB00002B/513